Kentucky Derby IQ: The Ultimate Test of True Fandom

JOEL KATTE

Printed in the United States of America.
Copyright © 2012 by Joel Katte.

All rights reserved. No part of this publication may be reproduced, stored in a retrieval system, or transmitted in any form or by any means, electronic, mechanical, recording, or otherwise, without the prior written permission of the author.

This title is part of the IQ Sports History / Trivia Series, which is a trademark owned by Black Mesa Publishing, LLC.

Cataloging-in-Publication Data is available from the Library of Congress.

ISBN: 978-0-9883648-1-3
First edition, first printing.

Cover photo courtesy of Susan Black.
Cover design by Holly Walden Ross.

Black Mesa Publishing, LLC
Florida
Black.Mesa.Publishing@gmail.com

www.blackmesabooks.com

Also by Joel Katte

Milwaukee Brewers IQ: The Ultimate Test of True Fandom

St. Louis Cardinals IQ: The Ultimate Test of True Fandom, Volume I (with Larry Underwood)

Kentucky Derby

History & Trivia

CONTENTS

INTRODUCTION

SPYING THE TWIN SPIRES, hugging the rail, hearing the snap of the gate, the crowd takes a nervous deep breath in unison. The horses lunge, the jockeys crouch. Now the race for the roses is run and timelessness has begun.

Long-shot odds, winning tickets, record crowds, Hall of Fame statistics, and historical dates all add up to the "Most exciting two minutes in sports." Think you know Kentucky Derby history?

Think again.

This IQ Series book will test even the best horsemen and trainers who have been around the sport their whole lives.

Test your skills. Wrack your brain. It's the ultimate Kentucky Derby IQ test.

You might be slow out of the gate. Maybe you will lunge to an early lead but fade to finish last. Perhaps you will pace yourself but eventually realize you don't have the pedigree to compete in a Triple Crown race. Regardless of your performance, go back and reread each chapter, and memorize every fun, fascinating Derby fact. When you can answer 90% or more of the 260 questions, you have achieved ultimate fan status!

"If you can figure out a way to visit the backstretch of Churchill Downs for morning workouts during Derby week, any begging you had to do will be worth it. With trainers and clockers leaning on the rail, workout riders hurrying to grab their next mounts, grooms hosing off steaming horses, the sound of hoofbeats, and galloping horses emerging from the morning fog, this is heaven for the true aficionado … You are actually close enough to see the horses' breath and hear the rhythms of their exertion."

— Sheri Seggerman and Mary Tiegreen in *The Kentucky Derby: 101 Reasons to Love America's Favorite Horse Race*

1 MORNING WORKOUTS

EVERY GOOD RIDE STARTS with a good warm up. Walking, listening to the horse, and avoiding anything that feels like work are essential for an effective warm up.

The same holds true for this book.

Go at a pace that works for you. Push yourself but remember to pull back just enough to save whatever energy and adrenaline is needed for your glorious win-by-a-nose photo finish.

However, if you start cramping in warm-ups, it will likely be a grueling, humbling ride ...

QUESTION 1: The Kentucky Derby is always held on which day?
a)   The first Sunday in March
b)   The first Sunday in April
c)   The first Saturday in May
d)   The first Sunday in May

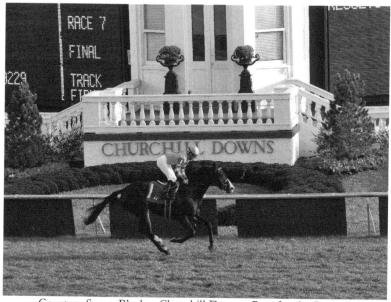

Courtesy Susan Black – Churchill Downs, Run for the Roses.

QUESTION 2: The first race was run in what year?
- a) 1870
- b) 1872
- c) 1875
- d) 1876

QUESTION 3: True or False: The Kentucky Derby is the last of the Triple Crown races.

QUESTION 4: Considered by many racing experts to be the greatest Thoroughbred of all time, this horse was born on March 29, 1917 in Lexington, Kentucky. He won 20 of his 21 career starts, including eight races in record time.
- a) Sir Barton
- b) Lexington
- c) Regret
- d) Man o' War

QUESTION 5: True or False: Kentucky Statesman Cassius Clay was one of the men who helped form the Commonwealth's first Jockey Club.

QUESTION 6: What three-year-old chestnut colt was the first Kentucky Derby winner?
  a) Hindoo
  b) Aristides
  c) Day Star
  d) Vagrant

QUESTION 7: Name the first horse to win the Triple Crown races: the Kentucky Derby, Preakness, and Belmont Stakes.
  a) Man o' War
  b) Lexington
  c) Regret
  d) Sir Barton

QUESTION 8: In 1925, *New York Times* and *New York Journal-American* sports columnist, Bill Corum, who later became president of Churchill Downs from 1950-1958, first used the famous phrase, "Run for the _____."
  a) Lillies
  b) Daisies
  c) Hills
  d) Roses

QUESTION 9: Name the 1973 Kentucky Derby winner who went on to become the first Triple Crown winner in 25 years.
  a) Secretariat
  b) Seattle Slew
  c) Affirmed
  d) Genuine Risk

QUESTION 10: What song is traditionally played by the University of Louisville Marching Band just moments before the start of the Kentucky Derby?

QUESTION 11: Name the Kentucky Derby winning horse that was purchased for $4 million by Fusao Sekiguchi at the Keeneland Yearling Sales.
- a) Big Brown
- b) Fusaichi Pegasus
- c) Barbaro
- d) Giacomo

QUESTION 12: This jockey who grew up in Colorado dreaming of becoming a cowboy, went on to be Kentucky's all-time leading rider at Churchill Downs and Keeneland. He once rode eight winners in one afternoon at Arlington Park in Illinois.
- a) Kent Desormeaux
- b) Pat Day
- c) Mike E. Smith
- d) Bill Shoemaker

QUESTION 13: Name the legendary basketball coach who is the lead partner in Celtic Pride Stable and the Ol Memorial Stable. HINT: He is best known for coaching the NBA's New York Knicks and Boston Celtics and the 1996 NCAA champion University of Kentucky Wildcats. Currently, he coaches for the University of Louisville. He is the first coach to take three different teams to the Final Four (Providence, Kentucky, and Louisville).

QUESTION 14: In 2011, this Team Valor horse won the 137th Kentcky Derby in front of a then record crowd of 164,858 with the help of jockey John R. Velazquez who was originally scheduled to ride the favorite and American Champion two-year-old Colt Uncle Mo before Uncle Mo was scratched due to an illness.
- a) Animal Kingdom
- b) Santiva
- c) Shackleford
- d) Twinspired
- e) Zenyatta

QUESTION 15: How old are all the horses that run in the Kentucky Derby?

Courtesy Susan Black – "Derby Dawn."

1 ANSWER KEY

1. C. The Kentucky Derby runs the first Saturday of May.

2. C. The first Derby was in 1875.

3. False. The Kentucky Derby is the first of the Triple Crown races.

4. D. Man o' War.

5. False. Not Cassius Clay! Rather, Kentucky Statesman Henry Clay helped establish the first Jockey Club, which became known as the Kentucky Jockey Club in 1809.

6. B. Aristedes was the first Kentucky Derby winner.

7. D. In 1919, Sir Barton became the first horse to win the Triple Crown.

8. D. Roses.

9. A. Secretariat.

10. B. Pat Day.

11. B. Fusaichi Pegasus was purchased for $4 million.

12. The Stephen Foster ballad "My Old Kentucky Home."

13. Rick Pitino. Pitino's best horses were Hallory Hunter 4th place at 1998 Kentucky Derby and AP Valentine winner of Champagne Stakes (2000).

14. A. Animal Kingdom. The first time Jockey Velazquez rode Animal Kingdom was in the Kentucky Derby and it was Velazquez's first Derby win in 13 tries.

15. All the horses that run in the Kentucky Derby are three-year-olds.

"The crowd in the grandstand sent out a volume of voice, and the crowd in the field took it up and carried it from boundary to boundary of Churchill Downs."
— *Louisville Commercial,* 1883

2 LAYING THE TRACKS FOR CHURCHILL DOWNS

PERHAPS IT ALL STARTED in 1779 when the 12th Earl of Derby and Sir Charles Bunbury saw the first running of the Epsom Oaks in England. Inspired, the two were determined to start their own race the following year. They flipped a coin for naming rights and Lord Derby won.

Years later when Kentuckians created their own version of the race using the Epsom Derby as the model, The Kentucky Derby was born and one of the richest histories in sports began.

You are likely to get a slow start out of the gate and may get blocked by the 20-horse, talented Kentucky Derby field. This is likely the toughest chapter in the book, so do not be discouraged.

Get to the rail and stay the course.

QUESTION 16: True or False: The first horse racetrack in Kentucky was in 1775 at Churchill Downs.

QUESTION 17: To avoid problems associated with racing in Louisville's busy downtown area on Market Street, a racetrack was created on Shippingport Island in 1805. Name the track that was on this island in the Ohio River.

    a)   Oakland Race Course
    b)   Hope Distillery Course
    c)   Elm Tree Gardens
    d)   Beargrass Track
    e)   Yum-Yum

QUESTION 18: What course was developed in 1827 on what is currently Main and 16th Streets?

    a)   Oakland Race Course
    b)   Hope Distillery Course
    c)   Elm Tree Gardens
    d)   Beargrass Track
    e)   Lynn's Paradise Course

QUESTION 19: Oftentimes races were held on private farms in the early 1800s. One of the more famous of these was Peter Funk's:

    a)   Oakland Race Course
    b)   Hope Distillery Course
    c)   Elm Tree Gardens
    d)   P. W. Reese Racetrack
    e)   Beargrass Track

QUESTION 20: "Old Louisville" boasts the site of this track that was opened in the fall of 1833. It was located in the area now known as Seventh and Magnolia Streets.

    a)   Oakland Racetrack
    b)   Hope Distillery Course
    c)   Elm Tree Gardens
    d)   Hunter S. Thompson Track
    e)   Beargrass Track

QUESTION 21: In 1858, Woodlawn Course opened on the Louisville and Lexington railroad near the area known today as East Louisville's St. Matthews. Although the track closed in 1870, the track's trophy known as the Woodlawn Vase is presented to the winner of what prestigious race?

Courtesy Susan Black – Churchill Downs, out of the gate.

QUESTION 22: In 1868, what harness racing track was built just east of Churchill Downs?
  a) Greeneland
  b) Keeneland
  c) Hope Distillery Course
  d) Zachary Taylor Track
  e) Beargrass Track

QUESTION 23: What is Colonel M. Lewis Clark, Jr.'s first name?

QUESTION 24: Clark was the grandson of what famous explorer and Missouri governor?

QUESTION 25: Colonel M. Lewis Clark traveled in England and France in 1872 and 1873. He met England's Admiral Rous and France's Vicompte Darn and other racing visionaries. How old was Clark when he first dreamed the idea of a Louisville Jockey Club that would ultimately lead to the development of Churchill Downs?

a) 26
b) 33
c) 46
d) 57

QUESTION 26: Where did Clark and other Louisville gentlemen meet on June 18, 1874, to discuss the development of the Louisville Jockey Club?

QUESTION 27: How many acres of land did M. Lewis Clark lease from his uncles John and Henry Churchill to construct a clubhouse, grandstand, porter's lodge, and six stables that eventually led to the opening of the tracks?
a) 40
b) 80
c) 110
d) 200

QUESTION 28: Clark financed the initial construction of the track by selling membership subscriptions to the track at $100 each. How many memberships did he sell?

QUESTION 29: Because the track faced financial woes, the New Louisville Jockey Club was incorporated in 1894. M. Lewis Clark remained as the track's presiding judge. Club President William F. Schulte constructed a $100,000 grandstand on the opposite side of the track. What is significant about this grandstand's architectural elements?

QUESTION 30: Clark modeled his three major stakes races after England's three prestigious races the Epsom Derby, Epsom Oaks, and St. Leger Stakes. What did Clark call his races?

QUESTION 31: True or False: Clark's three major races have been conducted in the spring since 1875.

QUESTION 32: Facing financial issues in 1902, a group consisting of Charles Price, tailor Matt J. Winn, and what Louisville politician began operating the track?

QUESTION 33: The first reference of "Churchill Downs" was reported in the *Louisville Commercial* in the ninth Derby in 1883: "The crowd in the grandstand sent out a volume of voice, and the crowd in the field took it up and carried it from boundary to boundary of Churchill Downs." However, the track was not incorporated as Churchill Downs until what year?
  a) 1885
  b) 1911
  c) 1919
  d) 1937

QUESTION 34: In 1918 and 1919, a group led by James Graham Brown took over Churchill Downs and what other three racetracks in Kentucky?
  a) Douglass Park, Latonia, and the Kentucky Association
  b) Keeneland, Greeneland, and Oakland Racetrack
  c) Lincoln Fields, Arlington, Red Mile
  d) Keeneland, Fairmount, and Douglass Park

QUESTION 35: What is the name of the association that took over Churchill Downs on January 16, 1928?

QUESTION 36: This association also served as the holding company for all of the following Kentucky and Illinois tracks except for which one?
  a) Douglass Park
  b) Latonia
  c) Lincoln Fields
  d) Arlington
  e) Washington Park

QUESTION 37: In 1948, President Matt Winn, other board members and a committee explored operating the track as a non-profit organization to donate its earnings to what institution?

QUESTION 38: Churchill Downs Foundation, a charitable organization led by J. Graham Brown, conducted several races each fall for charitable purposes resulting in in the donation of how much money during a ten-year period in the 1940-50s?

a) $250,000
b) $500,000
c) $1,500,000
d) $2,000,000

QUESTION 39: What Churchill Downs president took over for the retiring Wathen Knebelkamp in 1969 and lead the track in the 1970s and 1980s?

QUESTION 40: Who is William Whitley and why is he such a significant figure for Kentucky horseracing?

Courtesy Susan Black – Twinspired, practice run day before the Derby.

2 ANSWER KEY

16. False. Horse racing in Kentucky dates back to 1789. The first racetrack was created in Lexington.

17. C. Elm Tree Gardens.

18. B. Hope Distillery Course.

19. E. Beargrass Track.

20. A. Oakland Racetrack.

21. Since 1917, the winner of the Preakness Stakes at Pimlico has been presented the Woodlawn Vase trophy.

22. A. Greeneland.

23. Meriwether.

24. Colonel M. Lewis Clark, Jr. was the grandson of General William Clark of the Lewis and Clark Expedition. His father was Major Meriwether Lewis Clark, Sr. His mother was Abigail Prather Churchill.

25. A. 26.

26. The Galt House. In 2009, the Galt House Hotel, located on the waterfront of the Ohio River, signed a three-year sponsorship agreement with Churchill Downs to be named the "Official Host Hotel of Churchill Downs, the Kentucky Derby, and the Kentucky Oaks."

27. B. 80.

28. Clark sold 320 memberships at $100 each to finance the $32,000 track construction project.

29. The grandstand's twin spires constructed on the roof would become the symbol of Churchill Downs and the Kentucky Derby.

30. The Kentucky Derby, Kentucky Oaks, and Clark Handicap.

31. False. In 1953, the Clark Handicap began running in the fall.

32. In 1902, Mayor Charles Grainger was named president.

33. D. 1937.

34. Douglass Park, Latonia, and the Kentucky Association.

35. American Turf Association took over Churchill Downs in 1928.

36. D. Arlington.

37. University of Louisville School of Medicine.

38. C. $1,500,000.

39. Lynn Stone.

40. William Whitley was an American pioneer and an important figure in the early settlement of Kentucky. He fought in both the Indian wars and War of 1812, but his most significant legacy with Kentucky horseracing is that he laid out a racetrack in 1788 near present day Harrodsburg, Kentucky. Because Whitley vehemently opposed the British and disapproved of their customs, he insisted that his racetrack be opposite of theirs. The British preferred turf tracks, so he built his racetrack with clay, thus creating the first racetrack in America to consist of clay. Instead of running his races clockwise like they run in England, he ran his races counter-clockwise.

"With your throat dry from cheering ... you look down at the winning ticket in your hand, and no matter how large the payoff or whether you won by a whim or careful calculation, the greatest thing is to know you're still lucky."

— Sheri Seggerman and Mary Tiegreen, *The Kentucky Derby: 101 Reasons to Love America's Favorite Horse Race*

3 THE NUMBERS

WERE YOU SLOW OUT of the Chapter 2 gates? Don't fret. 2011 Derby champion Animal Kingdom went from last to first and you can too. At the very least, you can muster a respectable race the rest of the way and at least finish in the money!

QUESTION 41: How many people watched the first Kentucky Derby on May 17, 1875?
  a)   10,000
  b)   15,000
  c)   30,000
  d)   45,000

QUESTION 42: W. F. Schulte purchased the track in 1894 and built another grandstand. How high was this grandstand?
  a)   150 feet
  b)   215 feet
  c)   250 feet
  d)   285 feet

Courtesy Susan Black – Santiva, sixth in the 137th Kentucky Derby.

QUESTION 43: In 1896, the Kentucky Derby was shortened from 1 ½ miles to 1 ¼ miles. Why was the distance adjusted?

QUESTION 44: Of the first 28 Kentucky Derbys, how many were won by African-American jockeys?
- a) 5
- b) 10
- c) 15
- d) 26

QUESTION 45: In 1914, Old Rosebud set a track record of 2:03 2/5 and won the Derby by how many lengths?
- a) 5
- b) 6
- c) 7
- d) 8

QUESTION 46: In 1943, World War II travel restrictions prohibited Churchill Downs from selling tickets to out-of-towners. How many spectators witnessed Count Fleet, a favorite, pick up an easy win in what was called the "Street Car Derby"?

a) 50,000
b) 65,000
c) 70,000
d) 75,000

QUESTION 47: What were the odds for 1943 Kentucky Derby Winner Count Fleet?
   a) 2-5
   b) 4-5
   c) 1-1
   d) 2-1

QUESTION 48: Count Fleet went on to win the Preakness by eight lengths. How many lengths did he win the Belmont by?
   a) 8
   b) 12
   c) 18
   d) 25

QUESTION 49: How many stakes races did Citation win in 1948, the year he won the Triple Crown?
   a) 8
   b) 12
   c) 14
   d) 17

QUESTION 50: Col. Matt J. Winn, President of Churchill Downs from 1938-1949, died October 6, 1949, at the age of 88. How many Kentucky Derby races did he witness?
   a) 50
   b) 60
   c) 70
   d) 75

QUESTION 51: In 1974, the Derby celebrated its 100th race in front of a record crowd. How many people witnessed Cannonade win the 100th Kentucky Derby?
   a) 142,570
   b) 163,628

    c)   127,076
    d)   137,514

QUESTION 52: Longshot Ferdinand won the 1986 Kentucky Derby. What were the odds?
    a)   14-1
    b)   18-1
    c)   25-1
    d)   45-1

QUESTION 53: From 1980 until 1999, the crowd favorite had never won. That ended in 2000, when what favorite won to break the streak?
    a)   Monarchos
    b)   Charismatic
    c)   Funny Cide
    d)   Fusaichi Pegasus

QUESTION 54: About how many thoroughbreds are born annually in the United States?
    a)   13,000
    b)   24,000
    c)   34,000
    d)   56,000

QUESTION 55: Ben A. Jones holds the most Kentucky Derby wins by a trainer. How many times did one of his horses win the Derby?
    a)   4
    b)   5
    c)   6
    d)   7

Courtesy Susan Black – Uncle Mo, Breeders Cup racing.

3 ANSWER KEY

41. A. An estimated 10,000 spectators viewed the first running of the Kentucky Derby.

42. B. 285 feet.

43. The Kentucky Derby was shortened to 1 ¼ miles because 1 ½ miles was considered too long for three-year-olds to race so early in the cooler spring weather.

44. C. 15.

45. D. 8.

46. B. 65,000.

47. A. Count Fleet was 2-5 favorite and won by three lengths.

48. D. 25! Count Fleet's 25-length victory at the Belmont was a record that stood until 1973.

49. D. Citation won an astounding 17 stakes races!

50. D. 75. Winn witnessed each of the first 75 Derbys. At age 13, he watched his first Derby in the infield from his father's grocery wagon.

51. B. In 1974, a record crowd of 163,628 watched Cannonade top a field of 23.

52. B. 163,628.

53. D. Fusaichi Pegasus.

54. C. 34,000.

55. C. 6 wins.

"If I chose one horse and called him the greatest—that would start a controversy. But what sort of Irishman would I be if I didn't start a controversy, now and then? I chose Exterminator, because when greatness is reckoned, the factors entering it are speed, courage, stamina, intelligence, and perhaps, more importantly, durability."

— Mr. Kentucky Derby, Matt Winn (1945)

4 THE LEGENDS

ARGUMENTS ABOUT THE GREATEST horse and the greatest boxer of all-time will remain for centuries to come. However, I can assure you the most logical answers, in my humble opinion, will always reveal that both the greatest horse and the greatest boxer will be Kentucky-born and trained, and both will have run and fought the race or bout of their lives in Louisville.

QUESTION 56: What beloved horse legend was known as "Big Red"?
- a) Secretariat
- b) Citation
- c) Old Rosebud
- d) Red Auerbach

QUESTION 57: Who was the first filly to win the Derby in 1915? The win helped establish the Derby as one of America's premier sporting events.

    a) Zev
    b) Sir Barton
    c) Regret
    d) Exterminator

QUESTION 58: What horse won 20 of his 21 starts in 1919 and 1920 but never raced in the Kentucky Derby?
    a) Zev
    b) Sir Barton
    c) Man o' War
    d) Exterminator

QUESTION 59: This legend ran a 1:59 2/5 race to win the 99th Run for the Roses.
    a) Affirmed
    b) Secretariat
    c) Seattle Slew
    d) Spectacular Bid

QUESTION 60: What Triple Crown winner lost to another Triple Crown winner in the Marlboro Invitational Handicap?
    a) Affirmed
    b) Secretariat
    c) Seattle Slew
    d) Whirlaway

QUESTION 61: In 1983, this jockey finished the year riding 169 winners in the spring meet and 54 winners in the fall meet. Throughout this memorable season he rode five winners in a single day on five different occasions. His only Kentucky Derby win came in 1992 when he rode Lil E. Tee to victory. Name this legendary jockey.
    a) Bill Shoemaker
    b) Mike E. Smith
    c) Pat Day
    d) Chris McCarron

Courtesy Susan Black – Bodemeister, after the Derby race.

QUESTION 62: This legendary horse is one of only eleven Triple Crown winners. He set track records during his Derby and Preakness races and won 16 of his 21 races. Who is this legend?
- a) Gallant Fox
- b) Count Fleet
- c) Sir Barton
- d) Omaha

QUESTION 63: Name this horse who stumbled at the start of the Belmont, tearing away a part of his front hoof but somehow still managed to win by 3 lengths, equal the track record, and become the fourth Triple Crown winner.
- a) Assault
- b) Citation
- c) Whirlaway
- d) War Admiral

QUESTION 64: In 1986, legendary jockey Bill Shoemaker, became the oldest jockey to win the Kentucky Derby when he won with Ferdinand. How old was he?

a) 46
b) 48
c) 52
d) 54

QUESTION 65: On November 1, 1987, a statue of this legendary horse was dedicated in the clubhouse garden.
  a) Aristedes
  b) Hindoo
  c) Ben Brush
  d) Sir Barton

QUESTION 66: This legend defeated Triple Crown winner War Admiral by four lengths in the Pimlico Special of 1938.
  a) Johnstown
  b) Gallahadion
  c) Seabiscuit
  d) Bold Venture

QUESTION 67: Name the Triple Crown winning horse owned by Calumet Farm and trained by Ben Jones that exhibited a bizarre racing style that required Jones to create a blinker to prevent him from breaking to the outside rail.
  a) Sir Barton
  b) Whirlaway
  c) Citation
  d) Assault

QUESTION 68: What Triple Crown winner was never the favorite in any of the Triple Crown races?
  a) Sir Barton
  b) Whirlaway
  c) Citation
  d) Assault

QUESTION 69: This Triple Crown winner sired 10% stakes winners including Lady's Secret.
  a) Sir Barton
  b) Omaha

c) Citation
d) Secretariat

QUESTION 70: This large long-back colt won the Triple Crown and was buried at Nebraska's racecourse Ak-Sar-Ben in 1965.
a) Sir Barton
b) Omaha
c) Citation
d) Secretariat

QUESTION 71: In 1977, this horse became the tenth Triple Crown winner.
a) Affirmed
b) Secretariat
c) Seattle Slew
d) Whirlaway

QUESTION 72: Name the eleventh and last Triple Crown winner who won eight consecutive races in 1978.
a) Affirmed
b) Secretariat
c) Seattle Slew
d) Whirlaway

QUESTION 73: Name the only unbeaten horse to win the Triple Crown.
a) Sir Barton
b) Omaha
c) Citation
d) Secretariat
e) Seattle Slew

QUESTION 74: Jockey Gary Stevens was talking about what jockey when he said, "Someday he will be in the Hall of Fame, but he's already a legend among his peers"?
a) Mike E. Smith
b) Edgar Prado
c) Calvin Borel
d) Chris Antley

QUESTION 75: This grandson of 1893 English Triple Crown Winner Isinglass never won as a two-year-old and was sold to Canadian businessman J.K. Ross to be a running mate for Derby hopeful Billy Kelly. This horse was supposed to break early to wear out the field for Billy Kelly but he ended up going wire to wire for a remarkable win.

    a)   Sir Barton
    b)   Sir Huon
    c)   Pink Star
    d)   Plaudit

Courtesy Susan Black – I'll Have Another, making his move.

4 ANSWER KEY

56. A. Secretariat.

57. C. Regret.

58. C. Man o' War. Owner Samuel Riddle of the Glen Riddle Farm felt strongly that three-year-old horses should not have to run 1 ¼ miles in early May. Man o' War won the Preakness and Belmont in 1920.

59. B. Secretariat.

60. A. Affirmed lost to Seattle Slew. This was the first time in history that two Triple Crown winners raced against each other.

61. C. Pat Day.

62. B. Count Fleet.

63. D. War Admiral.

64. D. Shoemaker was 54 when he won the Derby with Ferdinand. Shoemaker said, "If Jack Nicklaus can win the Masters at 46, I can win the Kentucky Derby at 54."

65. A. Aristides, the first Kentucky Derby winner.

66. C. Seabiscuit.

67. B. Whirlaway.

68. D. Assault.

69. D. Secretariat.

70. B. Omaha.

71. C. Seattle Slew.

72. A. Affirmed.

73. E. Seattle Slew.

74. C. Calvin Borel.

75. A. Sir Barton.

"This is the day for anyone involved with horse. The dream is to win the Kentucky Derby, because there's nothing like it."
— Billy Turner, Trainer

5 THE DERBY WINNERS

THOUSANDS DREAM OF WINNING "The Run for the Roses" but every first Saturday in May, only one stands in the Kentucky Derby winner's circle.

In the infield, the winning horse and jockey are blanketed with the richest, reddest roses the Kroger florists could muster, and both enter the hallowed lore of winning horses and jockeys.

The Governor of the Great Commonwealth of Kentucky and the Chairman of the Churchill Downs Incorporated present trophies to the other members of the winning team, and the world stops and watches.

Of all the sights and sounds associated with the win, my favorite is the gleam in the horse's eyes and the bounce in its gait that seem to let everyone know that he, and sometimes she, knows that greatness was achieved.

QUESTION 76: What do Kentucky Derby winners War Emblom (2002) and Smarty Jones (2004) have in common?

Courtesy Susan Black – jockey Mario Guiterrez soaks in Derby glory.

QUESTION 77: With its ability to surge to the front late in the race, this colt was a crowd pleaser despite its lack of pedigree. It managed to win the 1961 Derby and Preakness.
  a) Carry Back
  b) Proud Clarion
  c) Tomy Lee
  d) Chateaugay

QUESTION 78: Name the horse who won the Kentucky Derby in 1951 despite its trainer skipping the race because he had such little confidence in the colt and Hall of Fame jockey Conn McCreary.

a) Iron Liege
b) Count Turf
c) Determine
d) Dark Star

QUESTION 79: Name the last Triple Crown winner.

QUESTION 80: What Hall of Fame horse finished second to a Triple Crown winner in all three of the Triple Crown races?

QUESTION 81: This 1984 Kentucky Derby winner was the son of Triple Crown legend Seattle Slew.
a) Sunny's Halo
b) Gato Del Sol
c) Swale
d) Pleasant Colony

QUESTION 82: Fusao Sekiguchi becomes the first Japanese owner to win the Kentucky Derby when this impressive horse won the 2000 Derby in front of 153,204 spectators. Name this Derby winner.

QUESTION 83: This 2001 Kentucky Derby winner finished with a remarkable 1:59.97 time.
a) Funny Cide
b) Real Quiet
c) Monarchos
d) Charismatic

QUESTION 84: On May 7, 2002, this horse died on his 25th anniversary of his Kentucky Derby win.

QUESTION 85: In 2003, this horse beat the heavily favored Empire Maker to become the first New York bred horse to win the Kentucky Derby.
a) Barbaro
b) Giacomo
c) Smarty Jones
d) Funny Cide

QUESTION 86: For the first time since 1983, this Kentucky Derby winner was featured on the cover of *Sports Illustrated*.
   a) Barbaro
   b) Giacomo
   c) Smarty Jones
   d) Funny Cide

QUESTION 87: Kentucky Derby winner Unbridled sired this 1996 Derby winner.
   a) Go for Gin
   b) Grindstone
   c) Sea Hero
   d) Thunder Gulch

QUESTION 88: Name the second filly ever to win the Kentucky Derby.
   a) Ruffian
   b) Genuine Risk
   c) Rachel Alexander
   d) French Arc

QUESTION 89: In 1985, this Kentucky Derby winner ran a 1:34 mile, which was the fastest mile in Derby history.
   a) Swale
   b) Sunday Silence
   c) Spend a Buck
   d) Ferdinand

QUESTION 90: What second-place Derby horse was the sire for 1987 Derby and Preakness winner Alysheba and 1989 Belmont winner Easy Goer?

QUESTION 91: What three horses did Hall of Fame jockey Gary Stevens ride to Kentucky Derby victories?
   a) Go for Gin, Grindstone, Super Saver
   b) Strike the Gold, Sea Hero, Street Sense
   c) Sunday Silence, Unbridled, Lil E. Tee
   d) Winning Colors, Thunder Gulch, Silver Charm

QUESTION 92: What horse won the 2008 Derby and the Preakness Stakes but was unable to win the Belmont to become the first Triple Crown winner since 1978.
   a)   Mine That Bird
   b)   Street Sense
   c)   Barbaro
   d)   Big Brown

QUESTION 93: This Triple Crown winner won the Kentucky Derby by 8 lengths and the Preakness by a neck. He was inducted into the Hall of Fame in 1964.
   a)   Assault
   b)   Omaha
   c)   Citation
   d)   Count Fleet

QUESTION 94: This horse became America's second Triple Crown winner. He set a single-season earnings record that was not surpassed for 16 years.
   a)   Sir Barton
   b)   Gallant Fox
   c)   War Admiral
   d)   Whirlaway
   e)   Count Fleet

QUESTION 95: Jockey Jose Santos rode what horse to 2003 Kentucky Derby and Preakness Stakes wins?
   a)   Funny Cide
   b)   Real Quiet
   c)   Monarchos
   d)   Charismatic

QUESTION 96: This New Mexico-based gelding rallied from last to win the 135th Kentucky Derby with the help of Calvin Borel getting to the rail after the break and sticking to it.

QUESTION 97: In 2007, Calvin Borel rode this horse to Kentucky Derby glory?

a) Smarty Jones
b) Barbaro
c) Super Saver
d) Street Sense

QUESTION 98: Nobody had heard of this underweight Venezuelan colt with a crooked leg who won the 1971 Kentucky Derby. The field was so large that the six weakest horses were grouped together on one wager. Name this horse that was in that group and went on to fly be all the favorites.

a) Cannonade
b) Canonero II
c) Majestic Prince
d) Dust Commander

QUESTION 99: This Kentucky Derby winner was known for running wide and frustrating everyone who worked with him. Trainer Ben A. Jones devised a one-eyed blinker that helped jockey Eddie Arcaro ride him to Triple Crown glory. Name this horse.

a) War Admiral
b) Whirlaway
c) Citation
d) Count Turf

QUESTION 100: This 2006 Kentucky Derby winner sustained a life-threatening injury at the Preakness. Fans tracked its progress by following hourly updates on the internet. After developing laminitis, he was euthanized on January 29, 2007. A statue of him racing to his Kentucky Derby finish was placed over his grave in front of the Kentucky Derby Museum outside Gate 1 at Churchill Downs.

a) Smarty Jones
b) Barbaro
c) Super Saver
d) Street Sense

QUESTION 101: What do Kentucky Derby winners Dark Star, Swaps, Kauai King, Riva Ridge, Bold Forbes, Spend a Buck, Winning Colors, and War Emblom all have in common?

QUESTION 102: This horse may have won the 1996 Kentucky Derby by a whisker. Name this photo-finish winner.
a) Silver Charm
b) Go For Gin
c) Grindstone
d) Thunder Gulch

QUESTION 103: This Kentucky Derby winner's hard luck story included the murder of his first trainer. The horse also shattered his skull and eye socket in the starting gate while training. Name this horse that became the first unbeaten Kentucky Derby winner since Seattle Slew.
a) Smarty Jones
b) Barbaro
c) Super Saver
d) Street Sense

QUESTION 104: A group of friends who purchased this Kentucky Derby-winning gelding arrived at the Derby in a rented school bus. The horse ran in between favorites Empire Maker and Peace Rules and won the 2003 Kentucky Derby.
a) Funny Cide
b) Real Quiet
c) Monarchos
d) Charismatic

QUESTION 105: Legendary jockey Mike Smith rode this horse to Kentucky Derby glory in 2005.

QUESTION 106: This horse won 21 of 22 races including the Preakness and the Belmont. His only loss was to Dark Star in the 1953 Kentucky Derby. Name this horse that is considered one of the greatest of all-time.
a) Count Turf
b) Needles
c) Native Dancer
d) Northern Dancer

QUESTION 107: Trainer Lynn Whiting and jockey Pat Day teamed up on this 1992 Kentucky Derby winner.

    a)   Lil E Tee
    b)   Forward Pass
    c)   Bold Forbes
    d)   Sunday Silence

QUESTION 108: Trainer Nicholas Zito and breeder Calumet Farm teamed up with this 1991 Kentucky Derby winner.

    a)   Winning Colors
    b)   Unbridled
    c)   Sunday Silence
    d)   Strike the Gold

QUESTION 109: Trainer Bob Baffert is known for Derby Winners Silver Charm, Real Quiet, and War Emblem. Name his two Kentucky Oaks winners.

    a)   Secret Status and Rachel Alexander
    b)   Silverbulletday and Plum Pretty
    c)   Rags to Riches and Blind Luck
    d)   Davona Dale and Lucky Lucky Lucky

QUESTION 110: This Kentucky Derby champion retired as the world's richest Thoroughbred, a record that was later broken by Cigar.

    a)   Alysheba
    b)   Big Brown
    c)   War Emblom
    d)   Funny Cide

QUESTION 111: The Myeyerhoff family paid $37,000 for this 1979 Kentucky Derby and Preakness winner, who won 10 of 12 races during his three-year-old season. One of the races he did not win was the Belmont; he finished third. He won 9 of 9 races his four-year-old season while setting four track records. Name this Hall of Fame horse.

    a)   Genuine Risk
    b)   Foolish Pleasure

c) Spectacular Bid
d) Spend A Buck

QUESTION 112: Riva Ridge was a two-year-old champion who won the Kentucky Derby. Before, Riva Ridge, how many years had it been since another two-year-old champion won the Derby?
a) 12
b) 16
c) 18
d) 20

QUESTION 113: In 1988, this horse became only the third filly in racing history to win the Kentucky Derby.
a) Regret
b) Genuine Risk
c) Winning Colors
d) Silverbulletday

QUESTION 114: This Canadian-bred 1964 Kentucky Derby winner sired 112 stakes winners.
a) Decidely
b) Northern Dancer
c) Proud Clarion
d) Lucky Debonair

QUESTION 115: In February of 2012, Kentucky Derby winner Animal Kingdom became the first Derby winner to do what since Giacomo in 2006?

Courtesy Susan Black – I'll Have Another, en route to 15-1 odds upset.

5 ANSWER KEY

76. Both War Emblom and Smarty Jones won the Derby and the Preakness but lost to longshots at the Belmont ridden by the same jockey Edgar Prado. Prado led 70-to-1 longshot Sarava to Belmont victory denying War Emblom the Triple Crown and also rode 36-to-1 Birdstone to Belmont victory denying Smarty Jones the Triple Crown.

77. A. Carry Back.

78. B. Count Turf.

79. Affirmed (1978).

80. Alydar finished second to Affirmed in all three Triple Crown races.

81. C. Swale, who also went on to win the Belmont Stakes. Sadly, Swale collapsed and died eight days after winning the Belmont.

82. Fusaichi Pegasus.

83. C. Monarchos.

84. Seattle Slew.

85. D. Funny Cide.

86. C. Smarty Jones was featured on the cover of the May 10, 2004 edition of *Sports Illustrated*.

87. B. Grindstone.

88. B. Genuine Risk.

89. C. Spend A Buck.

90. Alydar.

91. D. Gary Stevens rode Winning Colors (1988) Thunder Gulch (1995) and Silver Charm (1997).

92. D. Big Brown.

93. A. Assault.

94. B. Gallant Fox.

95. A. Funny Cide.

96. Mine That Bird.

97. D. Street Sense.

98. B. Canonero II. He went on to win the Preakness in the record time of 1:54.

99. B. Whirlaway.

100. B. Barbaro.

101. All eight horses were wire-to-wire winners.

102. C. Grindstone.

103. A. Smarty Jones. If it wasn't for Birdstone, Smarty Jones would have won the Triple Crown.

104. A. Funny Cide. He now resides in the Hall of Champions at the Kentucky Horse Park and is visited daily by fans from around the world.

105. Giacomo.

106. C. Native Dancer.

107. A. Lil E Tee.

108. D. Strike the Gold.

109. B. Silverbulletday and Plum Pretty.

110. D. Alysheba.

111. C. Spectacular Bid.

112. B. 16.

113. C. Winning Colors.

114. B. Northern Dancer.

115. Animal Kingdom became the first Derby Champ to win at four-years old since Giacomo. Animal Kingdom won at Gulfstream Park.

"No horse can go as fast as the money you bet on him."
— Nate Collier, cartoonist

6 MONEY, MONEY, MONEY, MONEY, MUNAAAAAA!

IN 1875 THE DERBY winner was guaranteed $1,000. In 1996, the winning purse rose to $1 million. By 2005, it reached $2 million.

Prime Minister of the United Arab Emirates Sheikh Mohammed bin Rashid Al Maktoum spends millions on his Thoroughbred Empire. In 2008, he spent $453 million to buy Bob Ingham's entire Woodlands Stud operation in Australia.

In 2005, Phoenix firefighter Chris Hertzog lost his Kentucky Derby superfecta winning ticket worth $864,253.50, the highest payout in Derby history. After two hours of searching through trash, he gave up hope. Custodial crews and others sifted through the track's garbage, with no luck. The next day, the mutuel clerk who sold him the ticket found it next to the machine that printed the ticket.

"Don't you just love happy endings?" Hertzog responded. Cha-ching!

QUESTION 116: What Kentucky Derby-winning jockey retired in 2005 with $297,912,019 career earnings?

a)   Mike Smith
b)   Eddie Delahoussaye
c)   Edgar Prado
d)   Pat Day

QUESTION 117: Name the Triple Crown winning horse that became the first horse to earn $500,000.
a)   Sir Barton
b)   Gallant Fox
c)   Count Turf
d)   Whirlaway

QUESTION 118: What year did Churchill Downs first turn a profit?
a)   1897
b)   1903
c)   1911
d)   1919

QUESTION 119: In 1911, the minimum bet was changed from what to what?
a)   50 cents to 25 cents
b) $1.00 to 50 cents
c) $2.00 to $1.00
d) $5.00 to $2.00

QUESTION 120: In 1913, this horse became the longest shot to win the Derby and pay $184.90, $41.20, and $13.20.
a)   Old Rosebud
b)   Donerail
c)   George Smith
d)   Exterminator

QUESTION 121: In 1922, a gold buffet service, including a loving cup and candlesticks, is presented to the Kentucky Derby winner. This was the first Derby presentation of its kind. What was the presentation's estimated value?
a) $700
b) $1,500

c) $7,000
d) $15,000

QUESTION 122: In 1938, the first tunnel under the track is completed from the grandstand to the infield. The infield presentation stand is also created and first used to recognize the Derby winner. How much did admission to the infield cost in 1938?
a) 25 cents
b) 50 cents
c) $1.00
d) $2.00

QUESTION 123: In the fall during the 1940s, the Churchill Downs Foundation, led by J. Graham Brown, held some races to raise money for charity. Approximately, how much money did the foundation donate during this ten-year stretch?
a) $250,000
b) $500,000
c) $1,000,000
d) $1,500,000

QUESTION 124: In 1959, Wathen Knebelkamp took over as President of Churchill Downs. Knebelkamp is remembered for his building and renovation projects. Improvement costs rose from $128,000 in 1959 to over $1,000,000 in 1966. He added 1,000 seats to the north end of the grandstand and built a museum in 1960. His addition to the fourth and fifth floors of the Skye Terrace is known as what?

QUESTION 125: In hopes of halting a stock takeover attempt, a group of Churchill Downs board members known as the "Derby Protection Group" successfully outbid National Industries for control, and the stock soared from $22 a share to what?
a) $25
b) $30
c) $35
d) $38

Courtesy Susan Black – an emotional win for jockey Mario Guiterrez.

QUESTION 126: In 1984, Thomas H. Meeker became president of Churchill Downs at age 40. He promptly began a five-year construction and renovation project that included the Matt Winn Turf Course, paddock construction, clubhouse renovations, barn area improvements, and Skye Terrance updating. How much did this five-year renovation project cost?
   a) $25,000,000
   b) $30,000,000

c) $35,000,000
d) $40,000,000

QUESTION 127: Name the 25-1 longshot horse that won the Kentucky Derby and paid $102.60, which at the time was the second highest payout in Derby history.
a) Mine That Bird
b) Grindstone
c) Giacomo
d) Ferdinand

QUESTION 128: The Kentucky Derby Gold Cup is a solid-gold trophy presented to the owners of the winning horse. It is created using a brick of 14 carat gold along with 20 carat gold accents. Diamonds were added to the trophies created for the 75th and 125th Derbys. What other jewels were added to the trophy presented to the winner of the 125th Derby?

QUESTION 129: This 100-1 longshot at the Travers Stakes defeated Triple Crown winner Gallant Fox.
a) Jim Dandy
b) Natchez
c) War Hero
d) Burning Star

QUESTION 130: How much did breeder August Belmont II sell Man o' War for at the 1918 Saratoga yearling sales?
a) $5,000
b) $15,000
c) $25,000
d) $50,000

QUESTION 131: Name the first horse to earn $1,000,000.
a) Assault
b) Burgoo King
c) Citation
d) Count Fleet

QUESTION 132: This Triple Crown winner earned over $1,000,000 and was purchased for the bargain price of $17,500.
    a) Gallant Fox
    b) Whirlaway
    c) Seattle Slew
    d) Secretariat

QUESTION 133: Seattle Slew sired 102 stakes winners for over $75,000,000 including all of the following except what horse:
    a) Swale
    b) A.P. Indy
    c) Capone
    d) Slew O' Gold
    e) Landaluce

QUESTION 134: How many of the first 136 Kentucky Derby post-time favorites finished in the money?
    a) 70
    b) 80
    c) 90
    d) 100

QUESTION 135: General Admission for the 137th Kentucky Derby was priced at what?
    a) $40
    b) $50
    c) $75
    d) $100

Courtesy Susan Black – I'll Have Another, alongside fourth place Went the Day Well.

6 ANSWER KEY

116. D. Pat Day.

117. D. Whirlaway.

118. B. 1903.

119. D. The minimum bet of $5.00 was changed to $2.00.

120. B. Donerail.

121. C. $7,000.

122. B. 50 cents.

123. D. $1,500,000.

124. "Millionaire's Row."

125. C. The stock rose from $22 a share to $35.

126. A. $25,000,000.

127. C. Giacomo.

128. Rubies and Emeralds.

129. A. Jim Dandy. After losing to Jim Dandy, Gallant Fox went on to win the Saratoga Cup, the Lawrence Realization, and the Jockey Club Gold Cup.

130. A. Samuel D. Riddle paid $5,000 for Man 'o War. This legendary horse retired with earnings of $249,465.

131. C. Citation.

132. C. Seattle Slew.

133. C. Capone. However, Seattle Slew did sire a horse named Capote.

134. C. 90. Although 90 of the first 136 post-time favorites finished in the money, since 1980 only eleven have finished in the top three and only four of those eleven have won.

135. A. $40.

"Only way that horses will win is if you sit there and spend time with 'em. Show 'em that you're tryin' to help 'em. Love 'em. Talk to 'em. You love 'em, and they'll love you, too."

— Eddie Sweat, groomer of Riva Ridge and Secretariat

7 THE TRAINERS

WINNING THE KENTUCKY DERBY is the highlight of a trainer's career. A select few trainers have won more than once. Sadly, some trainers win and set records throughout their racing careers, yet the coveted "Run for the Roses" eludes them time and time again.

QUESTION 136: In 2007, Todd Pletcher trained Rags to Riches who won the Oaks and also became the first filly to win the Belmont Stakes in 102 years! In 2011, Pletcher led all trainers in monies won. Name his horse that won him the Kentucky Derby in 2010.
   a)   Smarty Jones
   b)   Barbaro
   c)   Super Saver
   d)   Street Sense

QUESTION 137: This trainer was born and raised in Wisconsin and earned an education degree from the University of Wisconsin in Madison where he worked as an assistant basketball coach for two years. When he was off teaching during the summers he trained horses in South Dakota and eventually trained horses full-time. He went on to win four Kentucky Derbys including a 1999 win with Charismatic. He is tied with Sunny Jim Fitzimmons for the most Triple Crown wins with 13. Name this legendary trainer.

- a) Barry Hills
- b) D. Wayne Lukas
- c) Ray Hunt
- d) Jack Van Berg

QUESTION 138: What do trainers Bob Jones and James "Sunny Jim" Fitzsimmons have in common?

QUESTION 139: Name the trainer son of Ben A. Jones of Calumet Farm fame who won the 1957 and 1958 Kentucky Derby with Iron Liege and Tim Tam.

QUESTION 140: What trainer was only 24 years-old when his horse Hindoo won the Kentucky Derby in 1881?

- a) Ansel Williamson
- b) Edward D. Brown
- c) Edward Corrigan
- d) James Rowe, Sr.

QUESTION 141: Name the trainer who trained an astounding six Kentucky Derby winners.

- a) Tom Smith
- b) Max Hirsch
- c) Ben A. Jones
- d) Lucien Laurin

QUESTION 142: Who trained Kentucky Derby winners Winning Colors (1988), Thunder Gulch (1995), Grindstone (1996), and Charismatic (1999)?

- a) Bob Baffert
- b) D. Wayne Lukas
- c) Nick Zito
- d) Woody Stephans

Courtesy Susan Black – jockeys Martin Garcia riding Liason and Joel Rosario riding Creative Cause cool down behind Went the Day Well and I'll Have Another.

QUESTION 143: Name the father/son training team that trained Triple Crown winner Citation.

QUESTION 144: Name the only Kentucky Derby winning horse and trainer who shared the same name.
   a) Clyde Van Dusen
   b) Tom Smith
   c) Don Cameron
   d) Horatio Luro

QUESTION 145: What three Kentucky Derby winners were trained by Bob Baffert, one of the most famous American trainers?

QUESTION 146: In 1996, Baffert's horse Cavonnier lost by a nose to what Derby winner?
  a)   Strike the Gold
  b)   Grindstone
  c)   Sea Hero
  d)   Sunday Silence

QUESTION 147: Horseman Rick Dutrow won his first Kentucky Derby in 2008 training what memorable horse?
  a)   Big Brown
  b)   Mine That Bird
  c)   Barbaro
  d)   Giacomo

QUESTION 148: This Englishman trainer has a victory in the Belmont (1992) and seven Breeder's Cup wins. He trained Kentucky Derby winner Fusaichi Pegasus. One of his owners is Sheikh Maktoum. Name this legendary trainer.
  a)   Bennie L. Woolley, Jr.
  b)   Barclay Tagg
  c)   Nick Zito
  d)   Neil Drysdale

QUESTION 149: Born in a log cabin in Georgia in 1878, this Hall of Fame trainer trained horses for the United States Cavalry and later worked for C.B. "Cowboy" Irwin's Wild West Show, but he is perhaps best known for training Seabiscuit. Name this legendary trainer.

QUESTION 150: This son of Hall of Famer trainer Sylvester Veitch was born in Lexington, Kentucky. He is known for training Davona Dale, the 1978 three-year-old Champion filly and also is known for being the conditioner of Hall of Famer Alydar. Name this Hall of Fame trainer.

QUESTION 151: This Hall of Fame trainer's best horses were Count Fleet, Riva Ridge, and a special horse named Secretariat.
  a)   Tom Smith
  b)   Max Hirsch

c) Ben A. Jones
d) Lucien Laurin

QUESTION 152: This Brooklyn-born trainer has won all three Triple Crown races. Although he trained two Kentucky Derby winners Strike the Gold and Go for Gin, perhaps his most famous win was when Birdstone denied Smarty Jones the Triple Crown in the 2004 Belmont. Who is this legendary trainer?
a) Nick Zito
b) Neil Drysdale
c) Jerry Hollendorfer
d) Tom Smith

QUESTION 153: What Texan trainer is best known for Kentucky Derby winner Bold Venture and Triple Crown winner Assault?
a) Vince Lombardi
b) Miller Huggins
c) Max Hirsch
d) Red Auerbach
e) Henry Forrest

QUESTION 154: The "Gentleman Trainer" was born in Versailles, Kentucky, in 1921. As a teenager, he attended Keeneland Racetrack's first meet in Lexington, Kentucky in 1936. After spending time in the Air Force, he became a stable hand for Calumet Farm. He was known for his patience with difficult horses. His most notable champions were Epsom Derby winner Snow Knight and Kentucky Derby colt Sea Hero.
a) Frank McCabe
b) Buster Millerick
c) MacKenzie T. "Mack" Miller
d) Richard Mandella

QUESTION 155: Who is the winningest trainer in Kentucky with 271 wins at Churchill Downs and 153 wins at Keeneland?
a) Carl Hanford
b) Henry Forrest
c) James Conway
d) Thomas J. Kelly

Courtesy Susan Black – Animal Kingdom, surging forward.

7 ANSWER KEY

136. C. Super Saver.

137. B. D. Wayne Lukas.

138. Both Jones and Fitzsimmons trained two triple crown winners. Jones trained triple crown winners Gallant Fox (1930) and his son Omaha (1935). Fitzsimmons trained Whirlaway (1941) and Citation (1948).

139. A. Jimmy Jones.

140. D. James Rowe, Sr.

141. C. Ben A. Jones.

142. B. D. Wayne Lukas who is in the Museum's Hall of Champions.

143. Ben and Jimmy Jones.

144. A. Clyde Van Dusen (1929) Both winning horse and trainer shared the same name. Supposedly, Mr. Van Dusen did not name the horse. Rather, the horse, a son of Man o' War, was named by its breeder and owner Herbert Gardner. "Clyde is a little horse, and that is why Mr. Gardner named him after me," said Van Dusen, a former jockey. Mr. Van Dusen ended up owning the Derby winner Clyde Van Dusen after his racing career; he used him as an exercise pony.

145. Baffert's Derby winners are War Emblem (2002) Real Quiet (1998) Silver Charm (1997).

146. B. Grindstone. With photo finishes like that, no wonder Baffert's hair is white.

147. A. Big Brown, who went on to win the Preakness but finished a disappointing last at the Belmont Stakes. Dutrow is also known for training three Breeder's Cup winners.

148. D. Neil Drysdale.

149. Tom Smith.

150. John Veitch.

151. D. Lucien Laurin.

152. A. Nick Zito.

153. C. Max Hirsch.

154. C. MacKenzie T. "Mack" Miller.

155. B. Henry Forrest. Legend has it that Forrest watched the Kentucky Derby from a roof of a barn at Churchill Downs and told his friends that someday he would be in a Derby trophy presentation. Forty-five years later his prediction came true with Derby winner Kauai King. A couple years later he won the Derby again with Forward Pass.

"Bill Shoemaker didn't ride a horse, he joined them. Most riders beat horses as if they were guards in slave-labor camps. Shoe treated them as if he were asking them to dance."
— Jim Murray, *Los Angeles Times*

8 THE JOCKEYS

MARK PAUL IN HIS article "Top Kentucky Derby Jockeys" wrote: "The Kentucky Derby has a rich history. Everyone remembers some of the great horses that won the race. Many people think about the trainers as well. But what about the jockey? Jockeys don't always get enough credit when it comes to horse racing, but they deserve it. The actions of a jockey go a long way in determining who might win the race."

QUESTION 156: Name the small 50-1 longshot horse and its courageous jockey that passed 18 horses in the last half mile to win the 2009 Kentucky Derby in arguably one of the gutsiest rides of all-time.

QUESTION 157: What jockey rode Aristides to win the first Kentucky Derby in 1875?
   a)   Oliver Lewis
   b)   Billy Walker

    c)   Willie Simms

    d)   Isaac Murphy

QUESTION 158: How many African-American jockeys out of the 14 starters raced in the first Kentucky Derby?

    a)   8

    b)   10

    c)   13

    d)   14

QUESTION 159: Who is the last African-American jockey to win the Kentucky Derby?

    a)   Babe Hurd

    b)   Isaac Lewis

    c)   Isaac Murphy

    d)   Jimmy Winkfield

QUESTION 160: Who is the Hall of Fame African-American jockey who won Kentucky Derbys riding Plaudit and Ben Brush? He also was the only African-American jockey to win the Preakness when he won with Sly Fox in 1898.

    a)   Alonzo Clayton

    b)   Willie Simms

    c)   Isaac Murphy

    d)   Jimmy Winkfield

QUESTION 161: What was significant about jockey Jimmy Winkfield's Kentucky Derby wins on horses His Eminence and Alan-a-Dale?

QUESTION 162: Name the jockey who rode the 1913 91-1 longshot Derby winner to a then record time of 2:04 4/5? Hint: His nickname was the Golden Goose.

QUESTION 163: In 1897, Buttons Garner rode what horse to a Kentucky Derby win with 2:12.50 time?

    a)   Typhoon II

    b)   Pink Star

c) Flying Ebony
d) Stone Street

QUESTION 164: Frank "Shorty" Prior won the 1904 Derby riding what horse?
a) Judge Himes
b) Elwood
c) Wintergreen
d) Exterminator

QUESTION 165: Besides all having cool nicknames, what do jockeys James "Soup" Perkins, Fred "Buttons" Garner, and William "Smokey" Saunders have in common?

QUESTION 166: African-American jockey Willie Simms rode in two Derbys and won them both. He won aboard Ben Brush (1896) and Plaudit (1898) but he is perhaps best known for what accomplishment?

QUESTION 167: Hall of Fame jockey Johnny Loftus was known as a "first-class post rider, an excellent judge of pace, a powerful finisher, and an intelligent and capable handler of horses." He was the regular rider of two of the most famous Thoroughbreds of all time. Name these legendary horses.

QUESTION 168: Who is the rough-riding jockey who was suspended from racing after striking another jockey with his whip? Although this behavior was somewhat common during his era, he was never granted a license to ride again despite numerous appeals. Hints: He won the Derby in 1912 riding Worth. Despite his short and shady career, he was inducted into the Hall of Fame in 1970.
a) Arthur Pickens
b) Joe Notter
c) Carrol H. Schilling
d) Fred Taral

QUESTION 169: What was significant about Hall of Fame jockey Joe Notter riding Regret to victory in the 1915 Kentucky Derby.

QUESTION 170: Jockey William J. Knapp considered his 1918 Kentucky Derby win the biggest thrill of his career despite also riding Upset when they handed Man o' War his only loss in the 1919 Sanford Stakes. Name this Derby winner who gave Knapp his biggest thrill of his career.
   a) Bubbling Over
   b) Behave Yourself
   c) Morvich
   d) Exterminator

QUESTION 171: Twenty years into his career, this jockey rode Cavalcade to a Kentucky Derby win and considered that day to be the happiest day of his life.
   a) Earl Sande
   b) Mack Garner
   c) Willie Saunders
   d) Chick Lang

QUESTION 172: Name the Hall of Fame jockey who rode Kentucky Derby winners Morvich (1922) and Bubbling Over (1926).
   a) Albert Johnson
   b) Linus McAtee
   c) Eugene James
   d) Eddie Arcaro

QUESTION 173: Hall of Fame jockey O. Eric Guerin began his career at 16. Name the horse he rode to win the Kentucky Derby.
   a) Assault
   b) Jet Pilot
   c) Twenty Grand
   d) Hoop Jr.

QUESTION 174: This Kentucky-born jockey is best known for riding War Admiral to Triple Crown glory in 1937.
   a) Charles Kurtsinger
   b) Wayne D. Wright
   c) Conn McCreary
   d) Steve Brooks

QUESTION 175: Hall of Fame jockey Ivan H. Parke had a very short riding career (1923-1925) but managed to win 23.4% of his races. He trained 27 stakes winners including the 1945 Kentucky Derby winner. Name his Derby winning horse.
  a) Tim Tam
  b) Determine
  c) Decidedly
  d) Hoop Jr.

QUESTION 176: Hall of Fame jockey James Stout rode what horse to 1939 Kentucky Derby and Belmont Stakes victories?
  a) Shut Out
  b) Lawrin
  c) Johnstown
  d) Bold Venture

QUESTION 177: Who jockeyed 1943 Kentucky Derby winner and Triple Crown winner Count Fleet (1943) and also trained 1969 Kentucky Derby winner Majestic Prince?
  a) James Stout
  b) Willie Saunders
  c) John Longden
  d) Earl Sande

QUESTION 178: Name the first woman to ride in the Kentucky Derby.

QUESTION 179: What jockey won the 1950 Kentucky Oaks on Ari's Mona and then won the Derby the next day on Middleground?
  a) Warren Mehrtens
  b) Bill Boland
  c) David Erb
  d) Ismael Valenzuela

QUESTION 180: What do jockeys Eddie Arcaro and Bill Hartack have in common?

QUESTION 181: In 1966, Don Brumfield won the Kentucky Oaks riding Native Street. The next day he won the Kentucky Derby riding what horse?
  a) Proud Clarion
  b) Forward Pass
  c) Kauai King
  d) Chateaugay

QUESTION 182: How many Kentucky Derbys did Panama-native jockey Jacinto Vasquez win?

QUESTION 183: At 5-foot-1 and 117 pounds Laffit Pincay, Jr. was considered to be big for a jockey. He worked hard to maintain riding weight during his riding career that spanned from 1966-2003. Name the horse Pincay rode to a Kentucky Derby victory in 1984.
  a) Swale
  b) Spend A Buck
  c) Sunny's Halo
  d) Spectacular Bid

QUESTION 184: True or False: Pincay finished his career with over 9,000 wins.

QUESTION 185: Jockey William Hartack won on what 1960 and 1962 Kentucky Derby winners.
  a) Lucky Debonair, Venetian Way
  b) Decidedly, Carry Back
  c) Carry Back, Chateaugay
  d) Decidedly, Venetian Way

QUESTION 186: What year did Hall of Fame jockey Bobby Ussery ride Proud Clarion to a Kentucky Derby victory?
  a) 1966
  b) 1967
  c) 1968
  d) 1969

QUESTION 187: Who is the Hall of Fame jockey whose career ended in 1978 when he was paralyzed from an accident at Belmont Park.

He is remembered most for riding Secretariat from last to first in the Kentucky Derby and Preakness and also for winning the Belmont with Secretariat by 31 lengths.

QUESTION 188: In 1990, this jockey became the all-time winningest rider at Churchill Downs when he won his 926th victory.

QUESTION 189: Hall of Fame jockey Angel Cordero won three Kentucky Derbys and two Preakness Stakes. He considered his best ride to be Seattle Slew. His father was a jockey and trainer. Where was he born?

QUESTION 190: This Hall of Fame jockey from Panama rode Alydar to second-place finishes in all Triple Crown races in 1978. He rode Pleasant Colony to Kentucky Derby and Preakness Stakes wins in 1981.
   a)   Pat Valenzuela
   b)   Jacinto Vasquez
   c)   Jorge Valasquez
   d)   Gustavo Avila

QUESTION 191: Known as "The Greatest African-American Rider," this jockey is said to have won 628 of his 1412 races.

QUESTION 192: This Hall-of-Fame jockey has won over 5,000 races including Kentucky Derby wins with Real Quiet, Fusaichi Pegasus, and Big Brown.
   a)   Jose Santos
   b)   Jerry Bailey
   c)   Chris Antley
   d)   Kent Desormeaux

QUESTION 193: Jockey Mike Smith has won over 5,000 races but has only won one Kentucky Derby. Name the horse that Smith rode to Kentucky Derby glory.
   a)   Giacomo
   b)   Thunder Gulch
   c)   Monarchos
   d)   Grindstone

QUESTION 194: Name this racing Hall of Famer who has won over 6,000 races including a Kentucky Derby win with Barbaro in 2006.
    a)   Craig Perret
    b)   Stewart Elliot
    c)   Edgar Prado
    d)   Bill Shoemaker

QUESTION 195: At 17, this jockey led the nation in wins in 1977 with 487. He was the 1977 *Sports Illustrated* and *Sporting News* Sportsman of the Year. In 1978, riding Affirmed he become the youngest jockey to ever win the Triple Crown. Name this Hall of Fame jockey.

QUESTION 196: Name the Hall of Jockey who recorded over 7,000 wins, including Kentucky Derby wins with Alysheba and Go for Gin.
    a)   Gary Stevens
    b)   Pat Day
    c)   Chris McCarron
    d)   Bill Shoemaker

QUESTION 197: This iconic jockey was known as "The Iceman" because of his style of "sitting chilly," waiting just for the right moment before the ultimate push to finish line. Although he rode Whirlaway, he considered riding Seabiscuit the best of all. He helped Seabiscuit overcome a fourteen length deficit in the 1938 Hollywood Gold Cup. Later that year, he helped Seabiscuit beat War Admiral. Name this legend.

QUESTION 198: Name the Hall of Fame jockey who raved about riding Hamburg, the 1898 American Horse of the Year. Hints: Entertainer George M. Cohan wrote the patriotic song "Yankee Doodle Dandy" after him, and he is also best known for riding Clifford, Ornament, Voter, and Ballyhoo Bey.

QUESTION 199: Jockey William Shoemaker won on this 1965 Kentucky Derby winner?
    a)   Tomy Lee
    b)   Lucky Debonair

c)   Northern Dancer
d)   Iron Liege

QUESTION 200: Perhaps the most popular jockey of the twenties and thirties, this legend won 26.4% of his races! Poet Damon Runyon penned him the "Handy Guy." He won 39 stakes in 1923, including 10 on Zev, including the Kentucky Derby. He led Gallant Fox to Triple Crown glory and raced Crusader, Grey Lag, Billy Kelly, Mad Hatter, Sarazen, and Sir Barton, but considered Man o' War his best ride. Name this jockey immortal.
  a)   Albert Johnson
  b)   Linus McAtee
  c)   Johnny Loftus
  d)   Earl Sande

QUESTION 201: This Hall of Fame jockey led Hindoo to a 1881 Kentucky Derby victory and also won the Belmont Stakes a remarkable six times! Rival jockey "Snapper" Garrison stated, "He was the only jockey I hated to meet in an important race. He was a master judge of pace." Name this jockey.
  a)   Paul Duffy
  b)   Charlie Shauer
  c)   James McLaughlin
  d)   Billy Donahue

QUESTION 202: What legendary jockey won five Kentucky Derbys, six Belmont Stakes, and six Preakness Stakes? Hints: Although he rode eleven Hall of Fame horses, he considers Citation to be his best mount of all. He is the only jockey to win two Triple Crowns.
  a)   Eddie Arcaro
  b)   Bill Shoemaker
  c)   Conn McCreary
  d)   Bill Hartack

QUESTION 203: John Longden's riding career spanned from 1927 to 1966. In 1943, he rode Count Fleet to Triple Crown glory. His knack for getting horses to give their best performances earned him what nickname?

QUESTION 204: This jockey won five Kentucky Derbys. He rode Northern Dancer and Majestic Prince to Kentucky Derby and Preakness wins. Name this Hall of Fame jockey.
   a) Eddie Arcaro
   b) Bill Shoemaker
   c) Conn McCreary
   d) Bill Hartack

QUESTION 205: Name this jockey who won 8,833 races including 11 Triple Crown races. Hint: His Kentucky Derby wins came riding Swaps (1955), Tomy Lee (1959), Lucky Debonair (1965), and Ferdinand (1986).

QUESTION 206: Name the Hall of Fame jockey who won back-to-back Kentucky Derbys in 1982 and 1983 riding Gato del Sol and Sunny's Halo respectively.
   a) Eddie Delahoussaye
   b) Angel Cordero, Jr.
   c) Laffit Pincay, Jr.
   d) Jacinto Vasquez

QUESTION 207: Veteran jockey Mike Smith won his first Derby on long-shot Giacomo in 2005. How many Kentucky Derby races did he jockey before this memorable win?
   a) 7
   b) 9
   c) 10
   d) 11

QUESTION 208: This jockey known as "Milo" was the third of twenty-two children. He competed in races before his tenth birthday. He is best known for riding Tim Tam to Kentucky Derby and Preakness Stakes wins in 1958. He accomplished the same feat again in 1968 when he rode Forward Pass to win the first two legs of the Triple Crown.
   a) Bobby Ussery
   b) Braulio Baeza
   c) Ismael Valenzuela
   d) Hank Moreno

QUESTION 209: Kentucky Derby winner and Hall of Fame horse Majestic Prince was trained by what Hall of Fame jockey?

QUESTION 210: This son of a former slave is considered by many to be the greatest American jockey of all time. He is said to have won 44% of his races although 34.5% could only be verified in the chart books; however, in that era it is likely that some of the races were not documented in the chart books. He is remembered for his loyalty and honesty. Gamblers tempted him with bribes, hoping he would lose the 1879 Kenner Stakes; he refused and rode Falsetto to victory. Who is this jockey who was the first jockey inducted into the Hall of Fame and the first jockey to win three Kentucky Derbys?

8 ANSWER KEY

156. In 2009, jockey legend Calvin Borel showed true grit athleticism when he rode Mine That Bird to a remarkable Kentucky Derby victory. Borel and Mine That Bird finished the last half mile in 47.8 seconds. After the race Borel recognized his parents who had recently passed away.

157. A. Oliver Lewis.

158. C. 13.

159. D. Jimmy Winkfield.

160. B. Willie Simms.

161. Jimmy Winkfield's Kentucky Derby wins on horses His Eminence and Alan-a-Dale were significant because won them back-to-back in 1901 and 1902.

162. Roscoe Goose.

163. A. Typhoon II.

164. B. Elwood.

165. All three Kentucky Derby winning jockeys rode in the Derby only one time. Thirteen other jockeys have accomplished this feat. The first was Oliver Lewis in the first Derby in 1875 riding Aristedes. The last was Stewart Elliot aboard Smarty Jones in 2004.

166. Simms is the only African-American jockey to win all three races that became known as the Triple Crown. He was inducted into the Hall of Fame in 1977. The Thoroughbred Record noted Simms, "...has beautiful hands and is especially quick and clever in an emergency."

167. Sir Barton and Man o' War.

168. C. Carroll H. Schilling.

169. Regret was the first filly to win the Derby.

170. D. Exterminator.

171. B. Mack Garner.

172. A. Albert Johnson.

173. B. Jet Pilot.

174. A. Charles Kurtsinger.

175. D. Hoop Jr.

176. C. Johnstown.

177. C. John Longden.

178. Diane Crump rode Fathom in the 96th Kentucky Derby. Fathom finished 15th.

179. B. Bill Boland. Boland also went on to win the Belmont Stakes with Middleground.

180. Both Arcaro and Hartack won an impressive five Kentucky Derbys!

181. C. Kauai King. Brumfield and Kauai King also teamed up to win the Preakness Stakes.

182. Two. Foolish Pleasure (1975) and Genuine Risk (1980).

183. A. Swale.

184. True. Pincay finished his career with 9,530 wins.

185. D. Decidedly, Venetian Way.

186. B. 1967.

187. Ron Turcotte.

188. Pat Day.

189. Cordero was born in Puerto Rico, where he rode his first winner in 1960.

190. C. Jorge Valasquez.

191. Isaac Murphy.

192. D. Kent Desormeaux.

193. A. Giacomo.

194. C. Edgar Prado.

195. Steve Cauthen.

196. C. Chris McCarron.

197. George Woolf.

198. Tod Sloan. "Toddy" retired early due to judgments he faced for betting on his own races.

199. B. Lucky Debonair.

200. D. Earl Sande.

201. C. James McClaughlin.

202. A. Eddie Arcaro.

203. "The Pumper."

204. D. Bill Hartack.

205. Bill Shoemaker.

206. A. Eddie Delahoussaye.

207. D. 11. Giacomo was Smith's twelfth Kentucky Derby horse.

208. C. Ismael "Milo" Valenzuela.

209. John Longden.

210. Isaac Murphy.

"Horse sense is the thing a horse has which keeps it from betting on people."
— W.C. Fields

9 CELEBRITY SPECTATORS

ALL THE WAY BACK to famous Polish actress Helena Modjeska's attendance at the 1877 Derby, the rich and famous have been drawn to the Kentucky Derby. Celebrities from film, music, sports, and politics have been coming to the races since its beginning, and some have been so enthralled with the sport that they went on to become Kentucky Derby horse owners. Of course, some celebrities like Modjeska were impressed with the race but were most fond of the mint julep. M. Lewis Clark, founder of Churchill Downs, is credited with introducing Modjeska to the mint julep.

Picking a celebrity out of the crowd can be almost as exciting as picking a winning horse. A few Kentucky Derby spectators whose names are worth dropping include: Michael Jordan, Muhammad Ali, Babe Ruth, George Strait, Kid Rock, Tony Bennett, Morgan Freeman, Bob Hope, Raquel Welch, and J. Edgar Hoover. Oops, and I also should be sure to mention that Donald Trump and Paris Hilton are also on the Run for the Roses A-List.

Courtesy Susan Black – legendary jockey Pat Day, at the 2011 Derby.

QUESTION 211: The 1889 Kentucky Derby attracted what famous bank and train robber?

QUESTION 212: What celebrity below is not known to have attended the Kentucky Derby and watched from Millionaire's Row?
a) Madonna
b) Jack Nicholson
c) Kato Kaelin
d) Martha Stewart
e) Dennis Hopper

QUESTION 213: What Presidential candidate making his first Derby appearance observed a Derby winner disqualified for cheating?
a) Bill Clinton
b) Richard Nixon
c) Walter Mondale
d) Al Gore

QUESTION 214: Royalty have often attended the Kentucky Derby. The Earl of Derby came to the Kentucky Derby in 1930. Name the Duke who attended in 1951.

QUESTION 215: What Hollywood icon waved a cowboy hat as the grand marshal of the 1976 Pegasus Parade?

QUESTION 216: What rap star owned the 1992 Kentucky Derby third place horse Dance Floor?

QUESTION 217: Name the Major League Baseball team owner whose horse Concerto finished 9th in the 1997 Kentucky Derby.

QUESTION 218: Steven Spielberg was part owner of the horse Atswhatimtalknbout that ran in the 2003 Kentucky Derby. What place did Atswhatimtalknbout finish?

QUESTION 219: What famous actress from the 1934 classic film *It Happened One Night* attended a Kentucky Derby?
a) Mae West
b) Katharine Hepburn

   c)   Bette Davis
   d)   Claudette Colbert

QUESTION 220: Horseracing fan and stable owner Queen Elizabeth II fulfilled a lifelong dream when she attended the Kentucky Derby. In what year did she witness the Run for the Roses?

Courtesy Susan Black – Animal Kingdom wins the 2011 Kentucky Derby.

9 ANSWER KEY

211. Frank James, brother of Jesse James.

212. D. Martha Stewart.

213. B. In 1968, Richard Nixon was at the Derby when Dancer's Image's use of an illegal medication led to Forward Pass being declared the winner. Nixon was a guest of Governor Louie Nunn, and he became the first sitting President to attend the Derby when he returned to the race in 1969. Nixon vowed he would return to Churchill Downs if he won, the White House that is, not the race. He won and kept that campaign promise.

214. The Duke of Windsor.

215. John Wayne. At the Galt House, supposedly Wayne passed on bourbon and went with his favorite drink tequila.

216. Hammer, the artist formerly known as MC Hammer.

217. New York Yankees owner George Steinbrenner.

218. 4th.

219. D. Claudette Colbert.

220. 2007.

"A horse can lend its rider the speed and strength he or she lacks, but the rider who is wise remembers it is no more than a loan."
— Pam Brown

10 THE FINAL STRETCH

WITH THE FINISH LINE in sight, we come thundering down the final stretch with a few more fun facts, memorable moments, and other tidbits for you to share with your family and friends as you wait for your next Kentucky Derby post time.

QUESTION 221: What do Kentucky Derby winners Buchanen (1884), Sir Barton (1919), and Brokers Tip (1933) have in common?

QUESTION 222: The first Kentucky State Fair was held at Churchill in 1902. What spectacle drew a crowd of an estimated 40,000 to 50,000 people?

QUESTION 223: At the 1907 Kentucky State Fair, Churchill Downs featured what other kind of races?

QUESTION 224: Kentucky and what two other states dodged the "reform movement," which banned horse racing in Arkansas, California, Louisiana, and Tennessee?

QUESTION 225: When was the Derby first broadcast on network radio?
   a)   1922
   b)   1925
   c)   1927
   d)   1928

QUESTION 226: In the early 1930s, the first international radio broadcast of the Derby was transmitted from Louisville to Lawrenceville, New Jersey, and then to what English network?

QUESTION 227: In 1942, "Camp Winn" a tent camp consisting of troops gave Churchill Downs a memorable military touch. From where did the troops come from?

QUESTION 228: World War II travel restrictions caused this Kentucky racetrack to conduct its 1943 and 1944 meets at Churchill.

QUESTION 229: What threatened to snap the consecutive streak of Derbys at 70 in 1945?

QUESTION 230: What year was the Kentucky Derby first televised on national television?
   a)   1952
   b)   1953
   c)   1954
   d)   1955

QUESTION 231: "Film Patrol" was installed in 1954 in hopes of doing what?

QUESTION 232: Why was the winner's purse stripped from Dancer's Image and given to second-place finisher Forward Pass in 1968?

QUESTION 233: On November 4, 1984, a Churchill Downs crowd of 8,971 endured rain and cool temperatures to witness what for the first time?

QUESTION 234: What year did twilight racing begin at Churchill Downs?
   a) 1984
   b) 1985
   c) 1986
   d) 1987

QUESTION 235: What was significant about Ski Captain finishing 14th in the 1995 Kentucky Derby.

QUESTION 236: What is the name of the Churchill Downs mascot who was introduced in 1997?

QUESTION 237: Two days before the 2004 Kentucky Derby, a federal judge ruled that jockeys could do what?

QUESTION 238: Seattle Slew was undefeated when he won the 1977 Kentucky Derby. Name the next horse to win the Kentucky Derby with an undefeated record.

QUESTION 239: What Kentucky Derby horse owner also owned the NFL Houston Texans?

QUESTION 240: In 1938, the first of these were used at the Kentucky Derby, which soon become what many consider to be the most desirable Kentucky Derby collectible.

QUESTION 241: Who traditionally salutes the Derby winner with a toast at the Winner's Party after the race?

QUESTION 242: How old was owner Mrs. Francis Genter when her horse Unbridled won the Derby in 1990?
   a) 86
   b) 88
   c) 91
   d) 92

QUESTION 243: The Kentucky Derby Gold Cup is awarded to the winning horse's owner. What year was the first "trophy" awarded?

a) 1922
b) 1934
c) 1937
d) 1941

QUESTION 244: In 1924, Black Gold won and his owners were presented with the "Golden Jubilee Trophy," which is the current design given to today's owners. What change was made to the design of the trophy in 1999?

QUESTION 245: Name the last gelding to win the Kentucky Derby.
a) Tim Tam
b) Venetian Way
c) Hill Gail
d) Dark Star

QUESTION 246: In 1908, Stone Street won the Derby and set what mark that appears will hopefully never be duplicated?

QUESTION 247: What do the following Derby winners have in common: Halma (1895) George Smith(1916) Black Gold (1924) and Flying Ebony (1925) ?

QUESTION 248: What morning-line favorite finished third in the 133rd Kentucky Derby behind winner Street Sense and Hard Spun? Hint: He sired a foal nicknamed "Taco" with 2009 Horse of the Year Rachel Alexandra.

QUESTION 249: In the 2006 Preakness Stakes, Kentucky Derby winner Barbaro suffered a hind leg fracture that lead to his death. Name the horse that won the race. Hint: He sired Zenyatta's first foal.

QUESTION 250: Will we see Zenyatta and Rachel Alexandra 2012 babies in the 2015 Kentucky Derby?

Courtesy Susan Black – horse blanket, with Derby logo.

10 ANSWER KEY

221. All three horses entered the Derby Maidens, meaning they had not yet won a race.

222. A staged collision of two locomotives.

223. Auto races were held in 1907, 1908, 1910, and 1912.

224. New York and Maryland.

225. On May 16, 1925, Louisville's WHAS radio station broadcast the Derby on the radio for the first time.

226. British Broadcasting Company.

227. Fort Knox and Bowman Field.

228. Keeneland Racetrack.

229. The government's ban of horse racing nearly broke the streak of 70 consecutive Derby races; however, V-E Day announced the defeat of the Nazi war machine and the ban on horse racing was soon lifted. The 71st Derby ran on June 9, 1945.

230. 1952, CBS affiliate WHAS.

231. "Film Patrol" allowed racing officials to view replays.

232. Post-race testing revealed Dancer's Image had taken an illegal medication. This was the first disqualification of a Derby winner.

233. Fans watched racing on Sunday for the first time ever at Churchill Downs.

234. B. 1985.

235. Ski Captain was the first Japanese ridden and trained horse in the Derby.

236. Churchill Charlie.

237. The federal judge's ruling allowed jockeys to wear advertising during the Kentucky Derby and on race day. The Kentucky Racing Authority expanded the ruling allowing jockeys to wear advertising in all races in Kentucky.

238. Smarty Jones (2004).

239. Bob McNair.

240. Mint Julep Glasses.

241. The governor of Kentucky.

242. Owner Mrs. Francis Genter was 92 years old when Unbridled won the Derby in 1990.

243. A. In 1922, a gold buffet was awarded to winning horse Morvich's owner Ben Block. He also received a pair of candlesticks and a loving cup.

244. The horseshoe on the front of the trophy was changed to face upwards instead of downward for good luck.

245. B. Venetian Way (1960).

246. Stone Street won with the slowest time 2:15 1/5.

247. All four were black horses. Black horses rarely win the Derby. Remember that the next time you place your bet.

248. Curlin. He is a stallion at Lane's End Farm in Versailles, Kentucky. Rachel Alexandra and "Taco" reside at Stonestreet Farm in Lexington.

249. Bernardini. Zenyatta and her first foal live at Lane's End Farm. Zenyatta is expecting her second foal; this one sired by Tapit who has also sired 2011 two-year-old Horse of the Year and Breeder's Cup Juvenile champion Hansen. Rachel Alexandra is expecting her second foal; this one sired by Bernardini.

250. Only time will tell, but I would bet yes!

"Fourteen days after delivering what was considered a performance of a lifetime in the first leg of the Triple Crown, I'll Have Another laid his heart out in the stretch at Pimlico Race Course and now has pulses racing in anticipation of what could be a spectacular conclusion to this three-part series."
— Alicia Wincze Hughes, *Lexington Herald-Leader*

11 I'LL HAVE ANOTHER

ONLY ELEVEN HORSES HAVE won the Triple Crown of Thoroughbred Racing, winning the Kentucky Derby, the Preakness Stakes, and the Belmont Stakes. In 2012, it appeared the 34-year drought might end when Kentucky Derby and Preakness winner I'll Have Another began strutting his stuff and staring his opponents down at Belmont Park in Elmont, New York. However, tendonitis in his left front leg prevented the colt from running in the Belmont and led to trainer Doug O'Neill and owner J. Paul Reddam's decision to retire the horse that seemed destined for Triple Crown glory.

I'll Have Another was foaled by Arch's Gal on April 1, 2009 at Brookdale Farm near Versailles, Kentucky. He was sired by Flower Alley. I'll Have Another won $2,693,600 in career earnings. He started only seven races and won five. Reddam sold him to Shigeyuki Okada to stand on Big Red Farm on the Japanese island of Hokkaido.

This chapter takes us to the end of our Kentucky Derby history. Thank you for taking the Kentucky Derby IQ ride. Remember to stop and smell the roses and hold on tightly to all your winning tickets, for life is fleeting, but the Derby is every first Saturday in May.

QUESTION 251: In the final stretch of the 138th Kentucky Derby, I'll Have Another closed on Arkansas Derby winner Bodemeister's 3 length lead and went on to win by …?
   a)   A nose
   b)   ¾ length
   c)   1 length
   d)   1 ½ length

QUESTION 252: I'll Have Another's jockey Mario Gutierrez delivered a patient, poised, and masterful ride in his first ever Kentucky Derby trip. How old was Gutierrez when he won?

QUESTION 253: Bodemeister's second place finish was hailed by some as one of the best non-winning efforts the Kentucky Derby has ever seen. What horsing legend trained this horse?

QUESTION 254: Had Bodemeister won, he would have become the first horse since Apollo in 1882 to have accomplished what?

QUESTION 255: I'll Have Another became the first horse to ever win the Kentucky Derby out of what starting position?

QUESTION 256: How many spectators attended the 138th Kentucky Derby to witness I'll Have Another's spectacular finish? Hint: It was a record crowd.
   a)   162,457
   b)   164,231
   c)   165,307
   d)   169,326

QUESTION 257: I'll Have Another became the first Santa Anita Derby champion to win the Kentucky Derby since 1989. Name the 1989 Kentucky Derby Champion who won the Santa Anita Derby?
   a)   Sea Hero
   b)   Strike the Gold
   c)   Sunday Silence
   d)   Unbridled

QUESTION 258: Dennis O'Neill brother to trainer Doug O'Neill bought I'll Have Another for owner J. Paul Reddam as a two-year-old at the Ocala sale. How much did they pay for him?

QUESTION 259: Name the horse who ran down two-year-old Horse of the Year Hansen to win the $750,000 Bluegrass Stakes at Keeneland, finished third at the Kentucky Derby and was considered to be one of only a couple horses who had a chance to beat I'll Have Another at the Belmont.

QUESTION 260: Jockey Mario Gutierrez and I'll Have Another again ran down and snuck by jockey Mike Smith and Bodemeister to win the Preakness Stakes in what appeared to be almost a replay of the Kentucky Derby finish. Smith and trainer Bob Baffert took second place in all three 2012 Triple Crown races when they finished second behind Union Rags in the Belmont with what horse?

11 ANSWER KEY

251. D. 1 ½ lengths.

252. Gutierrez was only 25. Trainer O'Neill said, "This kid is just an ice-veined, cool, calm kid. He is very confident but humble." The young Kentucky Derby and Preakness-winning jockey and I'll Have Another's run at the Triple Crown reminded racing fans of jockey Steve Cauthen who was only 18 when he won the Triple Crown races with Affirmed in 1978.

253. Bob Baffert.

254. Had Bodemeister won, he would have been the first horse since Apollo in 1882 to win the Kentucky Derby without having run any races as a two-year-old.

255. 19th position.

256. C. 165,307.

257. C. Sunday Silence.

258. $35,000.

259. D. Dullahan who finished a disappointing seventh in the Belmont.

260. C. Paynter.

KENTUCKY DERBY IQ

250-260
You are among the horse racing world elite! Your Triple Crown winner status has you destined for the Hall of Fame. Enthusiasts will be talking about your record-breaking performance for generations to come.

200-249
You managed to win one of the Triple Crown races and a few more stakes races. You are able to retire on a lush farm in Kentucky, collecting a $150,000 stud fee for the rest of your life.

150-199
Your fast start is commendable but your stumble, torn ligament, and miraculous fight for your life won over the hearts of thousands of fans. People from all over the country come to visit you at Old Friends, a retirement home for Thoroughbreds in Lexington, Kentucky: www.oldfriendsequine.org

100-149
You never quite fulfilled your horseracing dreams of winning a stakes race, but you sure look like a racing legend. You are invited to the pre-Derby event "Dawn at the Derby" to warm up alongside a Kentucky Derby hopeful.

50-99
A respected sportswriter wrote that you are "Ferdinand the Bull of horseracing." You do still work sparingly at a riding farm, but most of your earnings come from parades and birthday parties.

0-49
Your performance is too painful to endure. Your suffering is too much to bear, so the agonizing decision to euthanize has been made.

ABOUT THE AUTHOR

JOEL KATTE IS an elementary school principal for Fayette County Public Schools in Lexington, Kentucky.

Joel loves taking road trips with his family. He and his family enjoy hiking, biking, swimming, and playing tennis. During summers, Joel also plays baseball for the Lexington Bombers in the Bluegrass Baseball League.

Joel will be donating 10% of his Kentucky Derby IQ royalties to the three-time Kentucky Derby winning jockey Isaac Murphy Memorial Garden in Lexington. For more information on the project visit:

http://www.sustainlex.org/immaghl.html

Joel's first book, *Milwaukee Brewers IQ: The Ultimate Test of True Fandom*, was a #1 best-selling baseball book on Amazon. In the near future he hopes to publish his memoir *The County Stadium Kid* along with more IQ Series titles. For updates follow Joel on Twitter @joelkatte or visit:

www.KentuckyDerbyIQ.blogspot.com
www.CountyStadiumKid.blogspot.com
JoelKatte@gmail.com

ACKNOWLEDGEMENTS

I **WILL BE FOREVER** grateful to Merle and Jeanne Hansen, the two most wonderful in-laws a man could have, for encouraging my wife and me to move our family to Kentucky. "You will not find nicer people in all the country," my father-in-law Merle says every chance he gets, "and you will not find a more beautiful state." And I need to extend an extra thank you to my mother-in-law Jeanne, perhaps the greatest aficionado of Kentucky authors, who encouraged me every step of the way asking politely and often, "When are you going to finish the book?"

Thank you Bill Whitman, manager of Calumet Farm, for taking two hours out of your workday to give my family a tour of your historic treasure. We will never forget meeting Ice Box, petting a few-days old foal, studying the pictures and trophies in your office, and visiting the cemetery of your farm's champion horses. But most importantly, thank you for sharing your farm philosophy that from day one, you treat every foal like it is a future champion. I have adopted that as the new philosophy of my school.

Susan Black, thank you for sharing your gift for photography with me and the readers of this book. The cover photo is captivating and sure to enrapture readers—to learn more about her amazing photos you can contact Susan: scblack2@aol.com.

To my colleague and friend Mark Chaplow, a Detroit Tigers fan horseman from Michigan whose passion for horses showed me firsthand that writing a book like this was worth it, I thank you.

I would also like to thank my publishers David Horne and Marc CB Maxwell for making me a part of their winning team. And Marc, I especially thank you for encouraging me with this book after I explained to you that our marketing plans for my Milwaukee Brewers IQ book went south with my move to Kentucky.

I would like to thank my Mom for picking up a bit of my marketing in Wisconsin after our move. Your pride in my first book made it easy to write a second. We miss you and love you dearly and cherish our visits with you.

To my daughters, Holly and Daisy, who showed me that a day at the races can be a bit of heaven on earth and equally as exciting as a day at the ballpark, especially with winning horses like Little Miss Holly and Daisy Devine to root for. Thank you, girls, for showing me that every day with you is truly a gift from God.

To my son Wesley, whose commitment and service to the Navy makes me more and more proud every day.

And last but certainly not least, I want to thank my beautiful bride Dawn who is and always will be the best thing that has ever happened to me. You are the funniest person I know, and your heart is as big as Secretariat's. Your love holds us all together. You are truly wonderbaar!

REFERENCES

WEBSITES
Derbyarchive.com
Derbymuseum.org
Docsports.com
Horseworlddata.com
Kentuckyderby.com
Kentuckyderby.info
Racingmuseum.org
Sports-quotes.com

PRINT
The Lexington Herald-Leader
The Kentucky Derby: 101 Reasons to Love America's Favorite Horse Race by
    Sheri Seggerman and Mary Tiegreen

ABOUT BLACK MESA

Look for these titles in the popular Trivia IQ Series:

- *Atlanta Braves*
- *New York Yankees*
- *Cincinnati Reds*
- *Cleveland Indians*
- *Boston Red Sox (Volumes (I & II)*
- *Milwaukee Brewers*
- *St. Louis Cardinals (Volumes I & II)*
- *Major League Baseball*
- *Mixed Martial Arts (Volumes I & II)*
- *Boston Celtics (Volumes I & II)*
- *University of Florida Gators Football*
- *University of Georgia Bulldogs Football*
- *University of Oklahoma Sooners Football*
- *University of Texas Longhorns Football*
- *Texas A&M Aggies Football*
- *West Point Football*
- *New England Patriots*
- *Buffalo Bills*

For information about special discounts for bulk purchases, please email:

black.mesa.publishing@gmail.com

www.blackmesabooks.com

Made in the USA
Middletown, DE
18 October 2014